A..B..C..
IMAGINE!
(SUPERHEROS
& VEHICLES)

A

WORKBOOK

A..B..C..IMAGINE!
A DOODLYCOUCH WORKBOOK
WWW.DOODLYCOUCH.COM
COPYRIGHT 2010
AMY S. MORGAN

USING YOUR IMAGINATION IS AWESOME!

EVERY ONCE IN A WHILE IT'S GOOD TO LET YOUR BRAIN FLOAT OFF INTO DREAMLAND AND SEE WHAT NEW THINGS YOU CAN COME UP WITH. USING YOUR IMAGINATION OPENS YOUR MIND TO A WHOLE NEW WORLD OF POSSIBILITIES.

THIS BOOK HELPS YOU TO DO JUST THAT. USING THE ABC'S AS A GUIDE, AND KIND OF A CHALLENGE, TRY TO COME UP WITH AS MANY IMAGINARY AND CREATIVE POSSIBILITIES AS YOU CAN.

THIS A..B..C..IMAGINE! WORKBOOK GIVES YOU A CHANCE TO DREAM UP A SUPERHERO FOR EVERY LETTER OF THE ALPHABET. FIRST YOU PICK THE DESCRIPTION OF YOUR SUPERHERO (AMAZING, BRAVE, CRAFTY), AND THEN YOU GIVE THEM A NAME (AL, BOB, CARL), SO YOU END UP WITH A SUPERHERO NAME STARTING WITH EACH LETTER (AMAZING AL, BRAVE BOB, CRAFTY CARL). AFTER YOU MAKE UP A NAME, THEN DRAW YOUR SUPERHERO USING AS MUCH IMAGINATION AS YOU POSSIBLY CAN. DO THEY HAVE WINGS, CAN THEY FLY USING MAGIC POWDER, CAN THEY HEAL PEOPLE WITH LIGHTBEAMS COMING FROM THEIR EYES? WHATEVER YOUR IMAGINATION CAN DREAM UP, THAT'S WHAT YOU CAN GIVE TO YOUR SUPERHERO.

THEN DO THE SAME THING FOR VEHICLES – WHATEVER YOU CAN IMAGINE, NAME IT AND DRAW IT. A CAR THAT CAN GO INSTANTLY TO INVISIBLE? THE INVISIBLE IT-MOBILE!

HAVE FUN! A..B..C..IMAGINE!!!

A_____(DESCRIPTION)

A_____(NAME)

DRAW YOUR SUPERHERO'S PICTURE HERE:

B_____(DESCRIPTION)

B_____(NAME)

DRAW YOUR SUPERHERO'S PICTURE HERE:

C _____ (DESCRIPTION)

C _____ (NAME)

DRAW YOUR SUPERHERO'S PICTURE HERE:

A..B..C..IMAGINE! SUPERHEROS

D_____(DESCRIPTION)

D_____(NAME)

DRAW YOUR SUPERHERO'S PICTURE HERE:

E_____(DESCRIPTION)

E_____(NAME)

DRAW YOUR SUPERHERO'S PICTURE HERE:

F_____(DESCRIPTION)

F_____(NAME)

DRAW YOUR SUPERHERO'S PICTURE HERE:

G_____(DESCRIPTION)

G_____(NAME)

DRAW YOUR SUPERHERO'S PICTURE HERE:

H_____(DESCRIPTION)

H_____(NAME)

DRAW YOUR SUPERHERO'S PICTURE HERE:

I_____(DESCRIPTION)

I_____(NAME)

DRAW YOUR SUPERHERO'S PICTURE HERE:

J _____ (DESCRIPTION)

J _____ (NAME)

DRAW YOUR SUPERHERO'S PICTURE HERE:

K_____(DESCRIPTION)

K_____(NAME)

DRAW YOUR SUPERHERO'S PICTURE HERE:

A..B..C..IMAGINE! SUPERHEROS

L _____ (DESCRIPTION)

L _____ (NAME)

DRAW YOUR SUPERHERO'S PICTURE HERE:

A..B..C..IMAGINE! SUPERHEROS

M_____ (DESCRIPTION)

M_____ (NAME)

DRAW YOUR SUPERHERO'S PICTURE HERE:

N_____(DESCRIPTION)

N_____(NAME)

DRAW YOUR SUPERHERO'S PICTURE HERE:

O _____ (DESCRIPTION)

O _____ (NAME)

DRAW YOUR SUPERHERO'S PICTURE HERE:

P _____(DESCRIPTION)

P _____(NAME)

DRAW YOUR SUPERHERO'S PICTURE HERE:

Q _____ (DESCRIPTION)

Q _____ (NAME)

DRAW YOUR SUPERHERO'S PICTURE HERE:

R_____ (DESCRIPTION)

R_____ (NAME)

DRAW YOUR SUPERHERO'S PICTURE HERE:

S_____ (DESCRIPTION)

S_____ (NAME)

DRAW YOUR SUPERHERO'S PICTURE HERE:

T _____(DESCRIPTION)

T _____(NAME)

DRAW YOUR SUPERHERO'S PICTURE HERE:

U_____ (DESCRIPTION)

U_____ (NAME)

DRAW YOUR SUPERHERO'S PICTURE HERE:

V _____ (DESCRIPTION)

V _____ (NAME)

DRAW YOUR SUPERHERO'S PICTURE HERE:

W_____ (DESCRIPTION)

W_____ (NAME)

DRAW YOUR SUPERHERO'S PICTURE HERE:

A..B..C..IMAGINE! SUPERHEROS

X _____ (DESCRIPTION)

X _____ (NAME)

DRAW YOUR SUPERHERO'S PICTURE HERE:

Y _____(DESCRIPTION)

y _____(NAME)

DRAW YOUR SUPERHERO'S PICTURE HERE:

Z_____(DESCRIPTION)

Z_____(NAME)

DRAW YOUR SUPERHERO'S PICTURE HERE:

A_____(DESCRIPTION)

A_____(NAME)

DRAW YOUR VEHICLE'S PICTURE HERE:

B _____ (DESCRIPTION)

B _____ (NAME)

DRAW YOUR VEHICLE'S PICTURE HERE:

C _____ (DESCRIPTION)

C _____ (NAME)

DRAW YOUR VEHICLE'S PICTURE HERE:

D_____(DESCRIPTION)

D_____(NAME)

DRAW YOUR VEHICLE'S PICTURE HERE:

ABC IMAGINE! – VEHICLES!

E_____(DESCRIPTION)

E_____(NAME)

DRAW YOUR VEHICLE'S PICTURE HERE:

F_____(DESCRIPTION)

F_____(NAME)

DRAW YOUR VEHICLE'S PICTURE HERE:

G_____(DESCRIPTION)

G_____(NAME)

DRAW YOUR VEHICLE'S PICTURE HERE:

H_____(DESCRIPTION)

H_____(NAME)

DRAW YOUR VEHICLE'S PICTURE HERE:

I _____ (DESCRIPTION)

I _____ (NAME)

DRAW YOUR VEHICLE'S PICTURE HERE:

J_____(DESCRIPTION)

J_____(NAME)

DRAW YOUR VEHICLE'S PICTURE HERE:

K_____(DESCRIPTION)

K_____(NAME)

DRAW YOUR VEHICLE'S PICTURE HERE:

L_____ (DESCRIPTION)

L_____ (NAME)

DRAW YOUR VEHICLE'S PICTURE HERE:

M_____ (DESCRIPTION)

M_____ (NAME)

DRAW YOUR VEHICLE'S PICTURE HERE:

N_____(DESCRIPTION)

N_____(NAME)

DRAW YOUR VEHICLE'S PICTURE HERE:

O _____ (DESCRIPTION)

O _____ (NAME)

DRAW YOUR VEHICLE'S PICTURE HERE:

P _____(DESCRIPTION)

P _____(NAME)

DRAW YOUR VEHICLE'S PICTURE HERE:

Q _____ (DESCRIPTION)

Q _____ (NAME)

DRAW YOUR VEHICLE'S PICTURE HERE:

R_____(DESCRIPTION)

R_____(NAME)

DRAW YOUR VEHICLE'S PICTURE HERE:

S_____(DESCRIPTION)

S_____(NAME)

DRAW YOUR VEHICLE'S PICTURE HERE:

T _____ (DESCRIPTION)

T _____ (NAME)

DRAW YOUR VEHICLE'S PICTURE HERE:

U_____ (DESCRIPTION)

U_____ (NAME)

DRAW YOUR VEHICLE'S PICTURE HERE:

V _____ (DESCRIPTION)

V _____ (NAME)

DRAW YOUR VEHICLE'S PICTURE HERE:

W_____(DESCRIPTION)

W_____(NAME)

DRAW YOUR VEHICLE'S PICTURE HERE:

X_____(DESCRIPTION)

X_____(NAME)

DRAW YOUR VEHICLE'S PICTURE HERE:

Y_____(DESCRIPTION)

Y_____(NAME)

DRAW YOUR VEHICLE'S PICTURE HERE:

Z_____(DESCRIPTION)

Z_____(NAME)

DRAW YOUR VEHICLE'S PICTURE HERE:

DISCLAIMER

COPYRIGHTS, TRADEMARKS & CREDITS

CONTACTING CORPORATE ELEMENTS, LLC

IF YOU HAVE ANY QUESTIONS ABOUT THIS DOCUMENT, PLEASE CONTACT:

AMY S. MORGAN
DOODLYCOUCH WORKBOOKS
CORPORATE ELEMENTS, LLC
AMY@CORPELEMENTS.COM
WWW.CORPELEMENTS.COM
WWW.DOODLYCOUCH.COM
PHONE (405) 326-4116

www.ingramcontent.com/pod-product-compliance
Lightning Source LLC
Chambersburg PA
CBHW081419280526
45788CB00009B/3164